TONY MATOS

# The Essential Guide to Navigate Your Proof of Concept

*Understand and implement practices to increase your Proof of Concept win-rate*

Second edition

This book was professionally typeset on Reedsy.
Find out more at reedsy.com

*To Gayla, Jason & Shantelle who make my life journey rich and beautiful. Thank you for the times we had, have now, and can look forward to together.*

*And to my faithful canine companion Molly who sat at my feet while I wrote this book – you are greatly missed.*

# Contents

## IV    Essential Realities

## V    Final Comments and Resources

# Foreword

Every journey is conceived as an idea but born with planning and action.

This publication began as an idea to contribute to the sales engineering community.

It is now in the hands of the presales community to shape and form this publication.

Tony Matos | January 2024

# Preface

## About Time | Peter E. Cohan, Author of Great Demo!

> This book really needed to be written — and now it really needs to
> be read...!

Far too many Proof of Concepts (PoCs) are run when they aren't required. Far too many PoCs are executed without sufficient structure for success. And far too many teams and organizations learn the hard way about PoCs, slowly and painfully reinventing the wheel over and over.

PoCs are one of the most expensive and resource-intensive sales activities. Not only that, but a PoC also represents one of the most costly and resource-intensive forms of proof for *both* vendors and customers. Entering into a PoC without a clear rationale, a clear plan, clearly defined success criteria, without agreement on the path to purchase, and a lack of approval on the roles of the participants and the timeline of activities — *is a recipe for enormous waste and ongoing frustration.*

If your sales team offers PoCs as a matter of convenience — this book will help correct or have you reconsider if that is the best strategy to use. If your PoC win rates are uncomfortably low, this guide will enable you to improve this KPI — perhaps dramatically. And if your PoCs suffer from delays, extensions, unclear results, and "no-decision" outcomes, you should turn immediately to page 1 and start reading...!

# Back to the Future | John Care, Author of Mastering Technical Sales

Indulge me in some "back in the day" memories. It is 1984, and a poor, overworked, and underpaid Sales Support Engineer (the title of the day back then) named John is getting ready to start a Proof of Concept. He visits the tape library, signs out a full set of the current production software, and walks out with six 9-inch magnetic tapes. Plus a 20-pound box of manuals/documentation and install guides. He throws them into the back of his car, alongside the second, secret, backdoor and personal "just-in-case" set of tapes he keeps for emergency use.

He then travels to the customer site, where (with luck) his onsite contact person has persuaded the IBM System Programmer to come into work before mid-day and install "foreign" software on his (in the 80's it was always a he) mainframe. Mount the first tape, type in some cryptic command, cross your fingers, and wait for the modules to load. Repeat until the pile of tapes is consumed. Verify the installation was clean and ensure you have sufficient security access, storage, memory, and administrative privileges. Then manually type in at least a half-dozen hexadecimal ZAP files (a.k.a patches) to fix bugs the development team deemed weren't necessary enough to resolve in their definition of production software. It was brutal. The Cloud was where your mind wandered while waiting for the tapes to load.

> That was the easy part — now we had to make everything work and look like magic.

Our PoC conversion rate (defined as successfully getting money from the client) varied from an incredible 80% for the US-East, Canada, and the UK down to a miserable 20% for the US-West and France. Why?

We had 89 global SE's and, therefore, 89 different ways of setting up and running a PoC. We had 134 salespeople, whose favourite phrase was "*oh, we can show you that in the PoC."* There was no such thing as SE Enablement, Sales Operations, or Regional SE Leadership – each district was on its own.

*"Someone should collect all these great ideas and processes (and also the bad ones) and write a book about it.."* we lamented.

Thirty-six years Later...we now have **The Essential Guide to Navigate Your Proof of Concept!**

# Acknowledgement

This book took shape amidst the challenges of the 2020 pandemic, a trans-formative period that left an indelible impact on our family, community, and nation. Much like countless others worldwide, we found ourselves profoundly affected by the inability to connect with loved ones and the loss of simple gestures, like greetings and hugs, that we once took for granted. These experiences revealed the profound importance of human connection and togetherness.

The pandemic served as a poignant reminder of our fundamental need for social interaction, highlighting the significance of valuing human aspects over mere reliance on processes and technology. This lesson extends beyond our daily lives and resonates even in the realm of executing a Proof of Concept (PoC).

The inspiration for this book draws heavily from the diverse roles in my career and the numerous individuals and organizations that enriched my journey as a sales engineering professional. Gratitude is owed to Steve Becker, who took a chance on me at Business Objects, and to Brian Baillod, my mentor during my initial venture into sales engineering. I must also acknowledge Mark Nolan for providing the opportunity to collaborate with talented sales engineering professionals at Citrix.

Many wonder if writing this book was a labor of love. The truth is, at times, it felt more like labor than love. Nevertheless, I am grateful for the crucial support that sustained me throughout this endeavor.

Special recognition goes to Peter E. Cohan and John Care for championing and endorsing the idea for this book, consistently urging me to "write the damn book." Their guidance, rooted in personal and professional leadership in the sales engineering community, proved invaluable.

Finally, heartfelt thanks are extended to my wife, Gayla. Amidst our busy lives, she not only encouraged me to undertake this project but also invested countless hours in editing the book. Editing work often goes unnoticed, but her dedication made this book readable. Thank you, Gayla, for standing by me and ensuring that this challenging yet rewarding project came to fruition!

# I

# Setting the Stage

*When embarking on a journey, it is important to understand the nature of the journey, the path, shortcuts as well as the pitfalls.*

*Having this understanding ensures we can enjoy the journey and arrive at our expected and planned destination.*

# 1

# Navigating a World-Class Proof of Concept

T o navigate a world-class Proof of Concept (PoC) requires a clear and pragmatic approach. This book serves as a roadmap for that purpose. This book has been written to read from front to back like a novel or utilize it to address specific issues. If you're new to the sales engineering domain or just embarking on Proof of Concepts, consider reading it cover to cover. If you're already familiar with PoCs but aspire to enhance your proficiency, select the chapters that will assist you in refining your skills.

I find that breaking down a journey into smaller segments aids in better planning. You will find that navigating a world-class PoC, we will also use the term evaluation in this book, can similarly be broken down into smaller parts. This book is organized into four stages:

1. **Setting the Stage:** Gain a comprehensive understanding of the intricacies and nuances of evaluations.

2. **Essential Milestones:** Familiarize yourself with the crucial markers at each stage of evaluations.

3. **The Essential Template:** Equip yourself with a template, a map, to ensure safe and wise navigation throughout the journey.

4. **Essential Realities:** Just like any journey, expect moments of drama and potential danger. Be aware of possible challenges so you can plan effectively.

This book was written to serve as a guide to *elevate your Proof of Concepts*, whether you're a novice or a seasoned presales professional, by providing a structured and insightful approach to the intricate world of sales engineering.

```
Now, let's take a quick look at what each of the four stages
brings to the table.
```

## Setting the Stage

In the role of a sales engineer, it's crucial to contemplate how we can establish a benchmark for effectively managing a Proof of Concept.

Proof of Concepts are widely recognized sales technique that significantly shapes a customer's perception of your solution. *Therefore, we require a structured methodology to steer the execution of a PoC.*

This book not only delves into a comprehensive range of topics related to executing a top-notch PoC but also reviews the purpose and audience of the book. Additionally, it introduces the foundational elements explaining why we employ a PoC.

## Essential Milestones

When embarking on a journey, having markers and signs to signify progress and direction is invaluable. In this stage, we present the *four indispensable milestones*, serving as navigational tools guiding your path toward a world-class PoC.

Each milestone is carefully outlined, emphasizing best practices to ensure the proper qualification, definition, execution, and closure of a PoC.

## The Essential Template

This section provides an in-depth review of the PoC Agreement Template. This template empowers you to articulate and manage a statement of work when conducting a PoC with a customer.

We define each section of the template, equipping sales engineers with a comprehensive understanding of what needs to be documented to execute a world-class Proof of Concept.

You can download a copy of this template for free - refer to our Final Comments and Resources section.

## Essential Realities

The final section addresses the topics and issues that a sales engineer must be aware of and manage during a Proof of Concept.

We explore subjects such as the importance of building customer relationships, discerning when and how to suggest alternative approaches beyond a PoC, and safeguarding against using a PoC as a pre-implementation for a production system.

The section concludes with a chapter on leading practices, drawn from both my personal experiences and those of fellow sales engineers during my tenure in presales.

# 2

# About This Book

## Setting a Standard

In my 36-year career, I devoted 25 years to being a presales professional. Throughout this extensive experience, I've witnessed the use of proof of concepts (PoCs) in various ways—*some good, some bad, and even some downright ugly.* It's important to note that the challenge of handling PoCs isn't exclusive to sales engineers.

While account executives, or whichever term is used to refer to sales leads, are often stereotyped as the ones prone to misusing a PoC, many of the account executives I've collaborated with demonstrate intelligent use of PoCs.

```
During my presales career, I've observed instances where PoCs were
misused by customers, account executives, sales engineers, and
yes, even myself. It's part of maturing in the presales role to
manage PoCs effectively.
```

Early in my career, I found myself grappling with the proper management of PoCs. Despite investing significant effort, my initial attempts didn't yield the crucial technical wins I sought. It dawned on me that the issue might not lie with the PoC itself *but rather with my approach.*

In due course, I realized that starting with my approach and self-improvement was key to effectively managing PoCs. I became aware of my lack of a clearly defined approach to PoC management.

Understanding this prompted me to change my approach to conducting PoCs. To enhance my presales career, I developed new strategies and methodologies over time, driven by the necessity for improvement. It's a learned experience to know what works and doesn't when it comes to a PoC. As such, regardless of your experience, it's possible to improve who you manage and navigate a PoC.

```
Invest the time to know which practices work best, and over time
your win rate will improve.
```

## Elevating our Game

In this guide, I advocate for a transformative approach among presales professionals—one that reshapes our mindsets and practices to enhance the execution of a Proof of Concept. When wielded strategically, a PoC is a powerful sales tool that should never be relegated to merely filling time while a sales strategy is formulated.

Recognizing this strategic value not only raises its significance in the eyes of customers but also exerts influence over when and how a sales team employs it to propel an opportunity toward closure.

Sales teams embracing this elevated perspective project a distinctive mindset and professionalism which fosters a deeper connection with their customers. There is a common perception that a PoC is a complimentary (free) engagement.

`Even though a customer may not pay for a PoC, it is far from free!`

As a presales leader, you must avoid giving a customer the sense that a PoC is free - a PoC has intrinsic value! As well a PoC requires a significant investment from a presales perspective. Everyone on the sales team must elevate the internal and customer perspective of leveraging a PoC. Elevating a PoC enhances your team's perceived importance in the eyes of the customer.

> *Let me emphasize this crucial point: You must reject the notion of a PoC being complimentary, succumbing to this viewpoint leads to a detrimental trap, consuming significant time and resources with minimal returns.*

I advocate for sales engineers to establish and uphold a higher standard when executing a PoC. A "world-class PoC" is characterized by specific traits:

- Understanding how a PoC fits within the account to advance the opportunity.
- Formulating a clear execution plan.
- Establishing a consistent feedback loop.
- Creating a published document as a statement of work.
- Employing project management practices to ensure timely and effective execution by the right resources.
- Setting success criteria before initiating the PoC.
- Designing the PoC with the customer's perspective in mind.
- Ensuring a PoC serves as an illustration, not an implementation.
- Showcasing your team and culture through the PoC.
- Leveraging the PoC to build lasting relationships and trust.

By embodying these and other principles, sales engineers can enhance the effectiveness of their evaluations while elevating their standing in the eyes of both the internal sales team and the customer.

# Purchase Order Coming

In this book, I often use the short-form "PoC" instead of spelling out "Proof of Concept" each time.

*However, there's an additional interpretation for the "PoC" short form:*
*"**Purchase Order Coming**"*

When a sales team agrees to a PoC, the objective should be a technical win that paves the way for a purchase order. By incorporating this alternative meaning, sales engineers can adopt a different mindset in approaching a PoC. It's crucial to emphasize that a successful PoC, or technical win, doesn't guarantee obtaining a purchase order.

Nevertheless, executing a PoC professionally and thoughtfully can enhance the likelihood of achieving a sales win.

# The Purpose of Executing a PoC

The primary reason for conducting a PoC is to win a customer over to your solution. As sales engineers, our focus during a PoC is on achieving the technical win.

```
A technical win is simply defined by a customer selecting your
solution over others. The hard part is acquiring the technical win.
```

While a technical win is a significant accomplishment from a sales engineering perspective, it doesn't automatically translate into a purchase order (sales win). Executing a world-class PoC aims to secure the technical win, to enable the account executive to progress towards the sales win – the point at which the customer decides to buy your solution.

It's worth noting that many technical wins occur without achieving the corresponding sales win.

> *The central theme of this book is to equip sales engineers with the skills to secure both the technical and sales win.*

Although this book doesn't delve into the sales processes, skills, and approaches necessary for obtaining the sales win, it asserts that a solid technical win positions the account executive for possible success.

## Sharpening the Saw

Knowing how to manage and execute a PoC is an essential presales skill set. When done properly it significantly influences how a customer perceives your solution.

> *Like any skill set, it requires continuous refinement and practice to remain sharp and effective.*

The analogy here is likened to a lumberjack's saw or axe, essential tools that must be regularly sharpened and cared for to minimize effort and maximize efficiency. A dull axe, similar to having few skills or approaches for conducting a PoC, results in significant effort with little to no results.

High-performing sales engineers must hone their skills to avoid unnecessary exertion when managing evaluations. This book aims to empower sales engineers to enhance their PoC engagement by refining their skills.

## The Pitfall of Familiarity

Sales engineer professionals must steer clear of the *trap of familiarity*, which can breed contempt. Familiarity may lead to the assumption that each PoC is identical to previous ones, potentially undermining its effectiveness.

It's so important that as the presales lead you show respect to each customer and don't assume this upcoming PoC is like the last few they did. We encourage you to shed the "dust of familiarity" and approach each PoC with a clean perspective.

## Method in the Madness

This book serves as a guide for sales engineers to effectively manage evaluations. It introduces a methodology covering:

- How to plan and think about a PoC using the four milestones.
- Understanding and engaging with PoC stakeholders.
- Using a standard template to document and manage a PoC.
- Leveraging a PoC to deepen customer relationships.
- Identifying when a PoC is veering off course and self-correcting.
- Recognizing when a PoC is not the proper approach to advance the opportunity.

```
A critical practice for every sales team is the adoption of a
methodology.
```

Knowing how to approach, think, and execute a proof of concept is essential for success. This book presents a methodology to enhance overall win rates by securing both technical and sales wins.

# 3

# Who This Book Was Written For

This book was crafted by a seasoned sales engineer with over 25 years of experience and is specifically tailored for sales engineers. Drawing upon a wealth of practical knowledge and real-world encounters, the concepts, processes, and content presented in this guide for executing a top-tier Proof of Concept are firmly rooted in genuine experiences rather than mere theoretical frameworks.

Through years of PoC endeavors and learning from mistakes, I have honed valuable insights into what truly works and have cultivated essential practices and a mindset to enhance your technical win rate.

In my early years as a sales engineer, like many starting in this field, I faced setbacks with some of my initial PoC attempts. These early failures spurred me to rethink my approach to PoCs. Over time, I refined my practices by observing successful strategies employed by fellow sales engineers. This amalgamation of learning from my setbacks, gaining insights from others, and coaching colleagues has allowed me to fine-tune a methodology.

*This methodology, applied by myself and others, has resulted in a noticeable uptick in our PoC win rates.*

This book serves as a comprehensive resource that the entire sales team can leverage to comprehend the intricacies of executing a world-class PoC. A cohesive sales team plays a pivotal role in defining success and elevating win rates, particularly during a PoC when team members must synchronize efforts to secure a technical win decision from a customer.

Although valuable for the entire sales team, the book primarily centers on the sales engineer, who bears the responsibility for the PoCs success. Consequently, while the guide offers insights applicable to the entire sales team, its primary focus is on the practices and processes crucial for sales engineers.

In the current landscape, sales teams exhibit various configurations, and organizational titles can vary widely. To provide clarity, let me outline some standard, albeit traditional, titles so that you can align them with your current role.

## The Sales Engineers

Sales engineers go by various titles, such as presales lead, sales consultant, technical sales, and solution consultant, among others.

```
The primary responsibility of a sales engineer lies in
understanding the inner workings of a solution and effectively
communicating its value.
```

To excel as a sales engineer, several key practices must be embraced. These include engaging in thorough discovery, conducting compelling demonstrations, possessing technical proficiency, and skillfully addressing questions and objections. These efforts collectively aim to ensure that customers gain a clear understanding of how a solution operates.

During a PoC, it is the sales engineer who brings the solution to life, quite literally putting "fingers to keyboard" to showcase its capabilities.

The success of a PoC is significantly influenced by a sales engineer's unique skills and their ability to engage with customers. Widely regarded as a trusted member of the sales team, the sales engineer plays a distinct role from that of an account executive.

```
While both roles are essential, customers perceive the sales
engineer as having a specialized and critical function.
```

Customers look to sales engineers to perform magic during a PoC by translating their requirements into a tangible, working solution. The active involvement of sales engineers in a PoC is crucial not just for functionality but also from an optics perspective. This centrality of the sales engineer in a PoC is driven by various factors, making their role pivotal in the overall process.

## The Account Executive

The role of an account executive, also known as the sales leader, salesperson, account manager, customer account lead, or relationship manager, is crucial in the sales landscape.

```
The primary function of an account executive is to be a "sales
leader" for an account. Their responsibilities encompass meeting
quotas, developing the sales pipeline, and taking accountability
for managing the principal relationship with the customer.
```

The active involvement of the account executive is paramount to the overall success of a PoC. Additionally, the account executive should be actively engaged in the qualification process of a PoC to ensure sufficient funding and executive support.

```
During a PoC, an account executive must not be passive or
disengaged.
```

Now, considering roles beyond the account executive and sales engineer, most organizations feature various team members in the sales function who contribute to opportunities or PoCs. While different organizations may have diverse roles within their sales teams, for simplicity and the objectives of this book, I will broadly categorize the sales team as comprising an account executive and a sales engineer.

# 4

# Foundational Elements

## What Are Proof of Concepts?

**W**hether you're embarking on your sales engineering journey or boasting years of experience, understanding the optimal instances to employ a Proof of Concept (PoC) is paramount for success in this role. This book not only outlines these best practices but also equips you with the discernment to make informed decisions on when to initiate or terminate a PoC.

In many organizations, the prevailing standard for PoC utilization is often dictated by the most vocal and accomplished account executive. However, this approach lacks the merit needed to establish a robust guideline or best practice.

To cultivate a culture of clarity, we must articulate well-defined best practices, methodologies, and frameworks for executing a top-tier Proof of Concept. Our starting point is comprehending the raison d'être of PoCs, deciphering the hallmarks of a successful endeavor, outlining the objectives, identifying key stakeholders, and ensuring their involvement to culminate in a purchase order.

# The Foundations of a World-Class PoC

Before delving into the nuances of how to assess, document, implement, and conclude a Proof of Concept, we must lay the groundwork with certain foundational elements.

Without these elements, any PoC risks deviating from its intended course. These foundational elements are pivotal in framing our mindset when entering into PoC discussions or engagements.

Here are essential features that underpin the execution of a Proof of Concept:

1. is pursued with the sole aim of winning business—*no ifs, ands, or buts.*
2. given the substantial costs associated with a Proof of Concept, judiciously allocate your resources.
3. implies a reciprocal relationship prevails—providing resources necessitates an expectation of reciprocation from the customer.
4. is an effective sales approach, it is not the exclusive one - alternative sales strategies exist, and careful consideration should be given to other sales tactics.
5. there are legitimate reasons to decline a PoC with a customer, and sales engineers must assert their stance when it is not the optimal solution.
6. requires focus and adherence to specific practices, methodologies, and mindsets which all contribute to a world-class PoC - sidestepping them for expediency invariably diminishes your success rate.

Let's look into each of these six features to understand how to manage a PoC.

## 01 | A PoC is To Win Business

In our pursuit of success, we commit to conducting a Proof of Concept (PoC) with a customer, aiming not only for a technical victory but ultimately securing a business triumph and a subsequent purchase order.

Understand this: there exists no other valid motivation for
engaging in a Proof of Concept!

Now, this perspective may differ from your current beliefs or the views of your fellow sales team members. If so, be open to the challenge presented in this book, urging you to contemplate adopting this mindset. Failure to do so might result in persistently conducting PoCs for the wrong reasons, perpetuating low success rates.

The transformation required isn't monumental; it commences with your acknowledgment that there are superior ways to navigate through a PoC. This book is designed to guide you in making that crucial shift in mindset, setting you on the path to enhanced success."

## 02 | Proof of Concepts Are Expensive

In the realm of sales, your organization must grasp and operate under the understanding that a Proof of Concept (PoC) comes with significant expense and risk!

This expenditure and risk are not limited to your sales team
alone; it also encompasses costs for your customer.

The pursuit of inadequately qualified opportunities incurs its own set of costs. This involves the commitment of a sales engineer to a PoC, diverting their attention from other potential opportunities. Additionally, there are time and resource investments tied to setup, equipment shipping, training, and education. Various teams, including sales management, legal, and accounting, may become engaged in the PoC process, further contributing to the overall cost.

Moreover, there is a tangible cost for the customer. Assigning personnel and departments within their organization becomes necessary, involving technical staff, business management executives, IT professionals, security experts, architects, business users, accounting, legal representatives, and purchasing departments, among others. All these contributions escalate the customer's expenditure associated with conducting a PoC.

It is crucial to dispel the simplistic and uninformed notion that a Proof of Concept entails little to no cost. If a customer holds such a view, it is the responsibility of the account executive to communicate otherwise. Similarly, if an account executive harbors this misconception, sales engineering management should intervene, enlightening them about the substantial cost involved in agreeing to a PoC.

Given that a Proof of Concept stands as one of the most financially demanding projects for a sales team in securing business, it necessitates thoughtful consideration and strategic decision-making on when to commit to a PoC with a customer.

## 03 | Quid Pro Quo - Give to Get

In my exploration of principles, I delve into the essence of a Proof of Concept, emphasizing the vital concept of giving to receive, often referred to as Quid Pro Quo. This Latin expression encapsulates the idea of an exchange, where one transfer is interdependent upon the other. Essentially, it signifies an agreement where you give something, but concurrently expect something in return.

```
Regrettably, it's a common scenario where sales teams furnish a
Proof of Concept without receiving anything in return.
```

To foster mutual benefits, it is imperative that both the account executive and sales engineer align themselves with the give-to-get approach. This ensures a symbiotic relationship that not only benefits them but also the valued customer. In the spirit of cooperation, both parties must be on the same page to optimize the outcomes of this reciprocal exchange.

## 04 | Why Are Proof of Concepts Still Used?

In the realm of solution vendors and customers, the Proof of Concept remains a widely embraced approach. Customers utilize a PoC as a strategic tool to delve into the intricacies of a solution, aiming to gain a comprehensive understanding of its capabilities.

> Given the substantial costs associated with the transformative nature of many solutions, making an informed decision at the outset becomes imperative for customers seeking sustained business growth.

The act of dismantling an existing solution can disrupt business operations, underscoring the importance of an astute decision-making process from the outset. Customers, therefore, need to navigate the landscape with a focus on risk minimization when contemplating an upgrade or the adoption of a new solution. Key aspects of risk mitigation encompass ensuring the solution's usability and acceptance among users, alignment with IT standards, adherence to security protocols, meeting required performance specifications, incorporating necessary features and functions from both business and technical perspectives, and gaining access to new capabilities that enhance business practices.

While a PoC can be integrated into the broader sales process of a solution vendor, it is essential to recognize that it is not the sole path to securing a deal. Another compelling reason to consider a PoC is to proactively engage with a customer before a competitor captures their attention. However, caution is advised in employing this tactic, as using a PoC solely to block a competitor may incur higher costs compared to alternative strategies for stalling competitors. Nevertheless, there are instances where a well-crafted PoC proposal can effectively delay a competitor.

Furthermore, a PoC can be leveraged to highlight the merits of a solution, expediting the decision-making process and securing early acceptance. This strategy shares similarities with using a PoC to fend off a competitor. By strategically showcasing the value of the solution in meeting customer requirements, especially with the right customer and a clear technical advantage, a PoC can propel the customer towards a swift decision, effectively solidifying their commitment to the proposed solution.

*In essence, Proof of Concepts are indispensable for both customers and solution vendors, serving various purposes.*

Regardless of the specific objectives, the successful execution of a PoC demands meticulous consideration, collaboration, and strategic planning before any agreement is reached. This approach aligns with the principles often advocated by leading presales professionals who emphasize the significance of thoughtful deliberation and proactive planning in navigating business endeavors.

## 05 | Reasons for Not Doing a PoC

When considering a Proof of Concept (PoC), it's crucial to weigh the reasons for and against initiating one. While there are valid motivations, such as genuine customer interest in trying out your solution, it's essential to discern the purpose behind the request.

Often, customers seek a PoC out of a desire for exploration and curiosity rather than a genuine business need or intent to make a purchase. This type of request tends to be more of a casual inquiry, akin to "tire-kicking," rather than a focused exploration of how the solution meets specific business requirements. While it's understandable that customers may want to explore and learn about your solution, a PoC may not be the most effective means for such endeavors. As discussed further in this book, there are alternative methods to enhance a customer's understanding of your solution.

```
It's important to recognize that a PoC isn't always the most
efficient way to move the needle in this regard.
```

Reasons to reconsider a PoC include situations where a customer fails to articulate their business needs, cannot introduce you to other decision-makers, lacks a budget allocation, or plans for implementation in the distant future. Be cautious of customers employing a PoC as a stalling tactic, especially those struggling with decision-making (experiencing paralysis by analysis).

Watch out for instances where customers use a PoC to deflect an account executive. Some customers find it challenging to decline requests, so they may resort to a PoC as a means to temporarily fend off an account executive. This can lead to sales engineers investing time in a PoC that won't result in an actual purchase.

It's advisable to refrain from suggesting a PoC to a customer solely in the hope of securing a sale. Adopting the mindset of "proof it and they will buy it" is akin to the "build it, and they will come" philosophy. While it may occasionally succeed, it's not a reliable practice. Account executives employing this approach risk diminishing the PoC win rate and jeopardizing other potential deals.

Solution vendors must cultivate the discernment to say YES to the right PoC while possessing the strength to decline the wrong ones. Building a robust sales strategy around a PoC involves strategic decision-making and a nuanced understanding of customer motivations.

## 06 | The Essential Elements of Success for a PoC

In this book, I delve into the core principles that constitute the best practices for executing a world-class Proof of Concept. While the text introduces various practices, tips, and methodologies, I want to highlight the essential elements that are indispensable for any successful PoC.

> A crucial factor in achieving a world-class PoC involves aligning the sales team with a unified approach and strategy.

Additionally, it requires cultivating curiosity and posing insightful questions to comprehensively understand the customer's situation. Collaboration, both internally within the sales team and externally with the customer, is paramount. Furthermore, placing value on documenting the PoC process and establishing well-defined success criteria contribute significantly. All these elements must unfold within a predefined timeline, with the sales team possessing a clear understanding of the "path to purchase."

While this book explores more essential elements in detail, these aforementioned aspects serve as the foundational pillars of a world-class PoC. I will elaborate on these elements later in the book.

It is crucial to note that a lack of clarity in these essential components poses a risk to your Proof of Concept, jeopardizing the achievement of your goal—to have a customer select and purchase your solution.

# 5

# What's in A Name?

To provide clarity in this book, it is crucial to establish clear definitions for the terms and processes associated with the implementation of "proof of concepts." The sales engineering community employs various naming conventions that can sometimes overlap. Additionally, alternative practices are employed instead of an actual "proof of concept."

This book addresses techniques such as Proof of Concept, Proof of Value, Trial or Evaluation, and a Pilot. While Technical/Architecture Reviews and Executive Briefings are not typically substituted for a PoC, it is important to comprehend their context and how they can enhance or impede a Proof of Concept.

What follows are the defined terms for each of these practices. These definitions serve as the foundation for the practices and methodology presented in this book.

## Proof of Concept

According to Wikipedia defines a Proof of Concept as:

> "... a realization of a certain method or idea to demonstrate its feasibility,

*or a demonstration in principle, whose purpose is to verify that some*
*concept or theory has the potential of being used..."*

Alternatively, a PoC can be described as a way to illustrate a set of specific requirements within a defined period.

A Proof of Concept is most effective with "out-of-the-box" software, allowing for quick value return. It is characterized by manageable customization, requiring moderate to zero data preparation and migration.

During my presales tenure, I also recognized that each PoC is different. I view these different PoCs in *levels* based on the solution and the market a vendor sells into. Not all PoCs are large and complex, taking weeks or months to complete. With proper organization and a focused market, even enterprise-level solution PoCs can be completed in just a couple of weeks - if you are organized and plan well. We will cover this later in the book.

Since there is variation in the solution vendor community regarding the different types, or levels of PoCs, I have simplified and categorized the three PoC levels based on the amount of touch it requires, where "touch" refers to the quantity of engagement and time needed to achieve a technical win. The three levels include low-touch, medium-touch, and high-touch.

```
This classification aims to help identify the effort and scope of
a PoC, recognizing that differences in pace, approach, speed, and
cadence impact the dynamics of each PoC.
```

It's important to note that while these classifications aid in understanding differences and nuances in a PoC, it is not recommended to rigidly classify PoCs in this manner. Each PoC is unique, and awareness of these differences enables a sales engineer to effectively manage their distinct nature.

Efficiently navigating Proof of Concepts (PoC) across these three levels is essential for successful sales endeavors.

## Low-Touch PoC

Low-Touch PoCs are prevalent in high-volume sales environments, often observed in small startups or with inside sales and SMB teams. Here, speed is crucial, and a PoC Qualification Form is utilized to swiftly identify solutions.

The primary goal is to secure a technical win promptly, aiming for a turnaround of a few days to a maximum of 1-2 weeks. Red tape is minimal in this setting, and the purchase path involves the same individuals engaged in the PoC.

## Medium-Touch PoC

Moving to Medium-Touch PoCs, the focus shifts to a single department, commonly found in mid-size IT departments with established management structures. More time is invested in these PoCs due to the increased complexity of dealing with specific departments.

Best practices are applied for effective qualification and execution. The time frame extends to 4-6 weeks, allowing for a structured approach and the acquisition of necessary funding and approvals.

## High-Touch PoC

High-Touch PoCs are on a grander scale, involving large or multiple departments. These PoCs set the standard for the customer and come with a significant rise in complexity. Larger teams are engaged, and thorough qualifications are imperative to ensure a technical win.

Failing in a High-Touch PoC could result in losing multiple departments or even the entire organization. The time frame here extends from 8-16 weeks, reflecting the intricate processes and considerations involved in this high-stakes scenario.

## Proof of Value

In the realm of solution evaluation, it's essential to distinguish between a Proof of Value (PoV) and a Proof of Concept (PoC). Nevertheless, in my extensive experience, the nuances between them are often not significant enough to merit distinct definitions. The primary difference typically centers around the interpretation of "concept" versus "value."

Fussing over semantics and maintaining separate processes for PoV and PoC may not be necessary. The practices required to conduct either a PoC or PoV are often quite similar. Consequently, it is advisable to settle on a single term and consistently employ it within your team and organization.

## Trials & Evaluations

Moving on to trials and evaluations, these terms are frequently confused or interchanged with PoCs. Customers may request a trial, providing them access to your solution for a specified period, often on their terms. However, this approach can lead to limited success, as users gain access with minimal training, akin to test-driving a car without guidance from salespeople.

Imagine a scenario where you can take a new car from a dealership, drive it for a few days, and return it without providing any feedback to the salesperson. This parallels the common pitfalls of trials and evaluations in the context of solution sales.

In practice, customers might start exploring the software during the initial days of a 60-day trial, experience a prolonged pause, and only realize the impending trial ends near day 49. Sales engineers often make the mistake of renewing the trial, resulting in a customer who lacks a profound understanding of the solution, leading to a significant loss of time and opportunity.

```
Trials, by their nature, give control and decision timing to the
customer, sidelining the engagement of sales engineers.
```

Thus, in my experience, the limited value offered by trials for enterprise-scale solutions suggests they should be avoided or transformed into managed PoCs.

# Pilots

Pilots, on the other hand, resemble PoCs but require a higher level of commitment and rigor, serving as a precursor to implementation. They are particularly suitable for solutions involving specialized training or prolonged use before realizing value.

# Technical and Architecture Reviews

Technical and architecture reviews are vital in a customer's scrutiny of your solution, focusing on its design and integration with existing technologies. However, it's crucial to recognize that these reviews don't substitute or hinder a PoC; instead, they serve as necessary checkpoints.

Executive briefings play a pivotal role in introducing key decision-makers to your organization and solution. Whether held on-premises, at the customer's location, or remotely, these engagements showcase organizational commitment, facilitate discussions with experts, and foster relationships with peer executives.

Now that we have a common language and understanding in the context of this book let's move to discuss the essential milestones for executing and managing a world-class PoC.

# II

# Essential Milestones

*When embarking on a journey, it becomes crucial to have clear markers and signs that signify your progress and guide your direction.*

*In this segment, I present the four pivotal milestones as your navigational instruments, steering you on the path toward achieving a world-class Proof of Concept.*

# 6

# The Four Essential Milestones

I n navigating the journey of a Proof of Concept, there exist four essential milestones. Each milestone plays a pivotal role in ensuring a comprehensive understanding, qualification, documentation, and successful execution of your PoC.

Think of these milestones as guideposts along the road, pointing the way and measuring progress toward your ultimate destination. Much like markers on a roadway, these four milestones are designed to keep you on course, guaranteeing you reach the final destination of a well-executed, world-class PoC.

The four milestones are listed and summarized in the diagram below. Subsequent chapters will delve into the details of each milestone.

to determine if the PoC is the right sales strategy to advance and win an opportunity

**QUALIFY**

 by asking the right questions of the right people to clarify the focus and success metrics

**DEFINE**

 using the PoC Agreement Template to capture the essential elements for a successful outcome

**EXECUTE**

 by conducting an executive-level PoC Key Findings meeting to showcase the results and business value to the PoC stakeholders

**CLOSE**

The Four Milestones

These four milestones function as reliable markers to simplify the navigation process, guaranteeing your PoC not only achieves technical success but also secures a purchase order, marking the accomplishment of your intended goals.

For each milestone, I outline the requisite best practices that ensure that a PoC is not only qualified and well-defined but also effectively executed and ultimately brought to a successful close.

> In the pursuit of a successful Proof of Concept (PoC), these four key milestones serve as a clear roadmap, guiding the way for initiation, execution, and conclusion.

These milestones provide a structured framework for the sales team, offering insights on whom to engage, which questions to pose, and which processes and documents to address. This not only facilitates a smoother journey for the sales team but also ensures clarity for the customer regarding the PoCs direction and progression.

For the sales engineer, typically positioned at the core of a PoC, these four milestones act as a simplifying force amid what is often a complex landscape.

This includes navigating through people management, political dynamics, and technical intricacies associated with a PoC. The ultimate objective is to execute a PoC of exceptional quality, securing the opportunity by not just meeting but surpassing customer expectations. These milestones serve as a strategic compass for navigating the intricate path of PoC success. Subsequent chapters will delve into a comprehensive exploration of each milestone, providing a detailed understanding of their significance in achieving a world-class PoC.

Let's now look at each of these essential milestones in more detail.

# 7

# Milestone 01 | QUALIFY

## Overview

I n the pursuit of sales excellence, the **Qualify** milestone stands as a pivotal juncture, requiring the sales team to assess whether embarking on a Proof of Concept (PoC) aligns with the optimal strategic approach. The decision to commit to a PoC should hinge on its potential to propel an opportunity forward with greater efficacy and impact compared to alternative sales methods.

Imagine the **Qualify** milestone as akin to deliberations with your family about planning a trip. In the early stages, uncertainties linger regarding schedules, destinations, and budgets. Nevertheless, the notion of exploring the idea remains a reasonable discussion point. Similarly, the initial phase of a PoC represents an opportunity to either advance a sale or, from the customer's perspective, gain insights into a solution's capabilities.

This milestone yields dual advantages. Firstly, it mitigates the risk of initiating a PoC without a clear understanding of overarching success metrics. Secondly, it facilitates a seamless commencement of the customer relationship, enabling the demonstration of capabilities, cultural alignment, and collaboration, all while discerning the customer's specific requirements.

> *It's imperative to recognize that qualification does not always culminate in an unequivocal "YES."*

Rather, it is about accumulating evidence that supports a positive response to a PoC. No member of the sales team should succumb to external pressures, whether from customers, partners, or sales leadership, to hastily agree to a PoC.

Focus on the **Qualify** milestone centers on a comprehensive documentation of the business and technical rationale for a PoC. This entails addressing concerns, identifying gaps, and assessing risks. The guiding principle during this phase is to refrain from making assumptions and to meticulously probe every aspect.

Beware of the "familiarity trap," wherein past experiences may cloud the ability to pose essential questions specific to the current PoC. The key lies in adopting a fresh perspective for each new PoC, ensuring that vital information is captured, and demonstrating a professional commitment to understanding the customer's unique needs.

Best practices during the **Qualify** milestone involve not only thorough questioning but also robust team engagement and collaboration. Success in this phase necessitates alignment between the account executive and sales engineer, deciding to pursue a PoC as a collective endeavor.

Striking a balance between communication and team engagement is critical. Overlooking this milestone may lead to ill-advised PoC engagements or crucial misses, while excessive detailing may result in counterproductive decision-making. Synchronization between the account executive and sales engineer is paramount.

Avoid justifying a PoC for misguided reasons, such as lacking a clear sales strategy, assuming simplicity, or succumbing to external pressures. The antidote lies in disciplined questioning.

To maintain focus and approach each PoC with a fresh outlook, adhere to best practices: collect information swiftly, prioritize voice channels over text/email, and set time limits for milestone activities, allowing for extensions if necessary.

## The Proof of Concept Qualification Form

I created the **PoC Qualification Form** to aid sales engineers in better navigating the **Qualify** Milestone. I know what you are thinking - more documentation!

If that thought ran through your head - get rid of it. You must take time to capture and document the PoC. I suggest employing this form to gather crucial details about the Proof of Concept.

```
This form serves primarily as an internal document for the sales
team to compile information and assess the PoC with a customer.
But it can also be used as a control and sales asset with a
customer.
```

While there is some redundancy with the information captured in the PoC Agreement Template (we introduce that later in the book), the details gathered in this form can be seamlessly incorporated into your PoC Agreement Template. Nevertheless, the purpose of this form is to empower the sales team to gather essential information for determining the feasibility of agreeing to a PoC with a customer.

Many teams opt to automate this form for convenience and enhanced collaboration with their sales management. In addition to integrating this information into your CRM system, the form can be part of an internal review or approval process before advancing to execute a PoC with a customer.

For Proof of Concepts categorized as low or medium touch, this form can substitute the PoC Agreement Template, especially when the structured scope of the template may not be necessary. To ensure a successful Proof of Concept, it is imperative to utilize at least one of these tools to capture essential information about the PoC before embarking on the execution phase.

The decision to use either the PoC Qualification Form or the PoC Agreement Template hinges on the dynamics of your sales team and the complexity of the PoC being conducted—whether it falls under the categories of low, medium, or high touch.

Refer to the Final Comments and Resources section to acquire a copy of this form.

## Outcomes

In reaching the **Qualify** milestone, the paramount goal is to foster alignment within the sales team regarding the impending decision.

```
Two potential paths lie ahead: either proceed with the Proof of
Concept (Go) or opt for an exit (No-Go).
```

The determination between a Go or No-Go decision lacks a one-size-fits-all formula. Nevertheless, there exist reliable indicators and proven best practices.

Ultimately, the key lies in leveraging the collective experience and fostering collaboration through astute questioning of the customer. This approach empowers the sales team to arrive at an informed and strategic decision.

# Make a Decision!

Now that you've delved into the pertinent details outlined in the PoC Qualification Form, it's time to reach a decision!

Gather your team to collectively analyze the PoC information. Ensure the completed PoC Qualification Form is distributed beforehand, allowing everyone to come prepared. The objective of this meeting is not to get bogged down in minutiae but to make a practical, common-sense decision regarding the feasibility of the PoC.

The outcome of this meeting holds immense significance as it shapes your future trajectory. A poorly informed decision may lead to investing valuable time in a PoC when resources could be better directed elsewhere. Conversely, deciding to opt out due to insufficient information might mean missing out on a potentially significant opportunity.

Hence, it is crucial to conduct a focused meeting, guided by four key objectives:

1. **Set and Clarify Meeting Objective**: The account executive should articulate that the meeting aims to review the collected information, leading to a decisive Go or No-Go determination. Avoid delving into intricate technical or sales strategy discussions; focus on the PoCs viability and steer towards a resolution.

2. **Review the Evidence**: Engage in a robust discussion of the findings from the PoC Qualification Form to affirm what is known or unknown. Encourage vigorous debate while leaving egos and corporate positions at the door. While broader sales strategies may support pursuing a PoC, refrain from pressuring the team into a decision without sufficient evidence.

3. **Vote!** This process isn't about achieving consensus, as that can paralyze decision-making. Each team member has a single vote, and in the case of a tie, the account executive breaks it.

4. **Decision Next Steps**: Now, you face two decisions: a "No-Go Decision" signals that the PoC isn't the right fit for the opportunity, or a "Go Decision" indicates alignment with the sales strategy.

If there's insufficient information to decide, revisit the questions asked during discovery. It's better to clarify now than invest time and resources in a poorly defined PoC later.

```
If the customer remains unresponsive or evasive, consider it a red
flag--proceeding may not be in your best interest.
```

Regardless of the decision, document the rationale. This documentation serves as a valuable resource for future decision points. If the decision is a Go, proceed to the **Define** milestone, concluding the PoC qualification phase. Whether you decide to move forward or not, this marks a pivotal moment in your engagement with the PoC.

# 8

# Milestone 02 | DEFINE

## Overview

In the **Define** milestone, our goal is to gather and organize the specifics of the Proof of Concept (PoC). We're talking about the what, when, where, and how of bringing the PoC to fruition. How well we handle this milestone significantly impacts the overall outcome and direction of the entire PoC.

Setting the right course during the **Define** milestone is crucial. The way you define the scope and objectives here will directly influence the success of your PoC. Utilizing the PoC Agreement Template serves as the tool to capture the insights, discussions, and documentation gathered during this milestone.

```
This template becomes your vehicle for constructing the necessary
work statement to ensure a successful PoC with your customer.
```

When completing the template ensure you craft the document in plain language, making the PoC accessible to anyone while still encompassing the technical nuances relevant to the customer's environment and your solution. Achieve a balanced content mix that speaks to both business and technical participants. The document should be comprehensible to those not directly involved in the PoC, outlining issues, resolutions, and approaches.

Collaboration among the sales team, sales engineer, and customer is essential in creating the PoC Agreement document. A partnership approach not only enhances the document's quality but also strengthens the mutual relationship, trust, and respect with the customer.

the primary focus of the **Define** milestone revolves around discovering the fundamental elements, requirements, and outcomes essential for a successful PoC. Completion of this document signifies that both the sales team and the customer share a common understanding of what is needed to demonstrate a solution within the customer's context.

```
For the sales team, especially the sales engineer, this document
serves as the definitive statement of work, providing clarity on
what needs to be done and how to accomplish it during the PoC.
```

In terms of best practices, it's vital to establish the sales engineer as the chief editor and manager of the PoC Agreement. Often, an account executive's name is prominently featured on the agreement, implying authorship. This practice needs to change. The sales engineer is the owner and manager of the PoC, and therefore, their name should rightfully appear on the front cover.

## Avoiding Certain Behaviors and Practices

In navigating the **Define** milestone, it's crucial to steer clear of specific behaviors and practices that could impede progress toward a successful Proof of Concept completion. Left unchecked, these behaviors detract from achieving a successful outcome.

## Too Much Detail

In the **Define** milestone, excessive focus on intricate details can lead to overload. Remember, the purpose of a PoC is to showcase the value of your solution, not to implement it. To strike the right balance, a collaboration between an account executive and a sales engineer is essential.

Together, they should ensure sufficient detail for clarity without hindering the PoCs reasonable progression. It's vital to grasp that getting bogged down in detail hampers the journey to a purchase order.

## Scope Creep

Even with the avoidance of excessive detail, scope creep can occur. Failing to document essential details, such as solution success metrics and timeframes for PoC execution, increases the likelihood of scope creep. Managing this involves saying "NO" when necessary, and avoiding the "nice-person" syndrome.

Precision in responding, explaining why certain requests are not feasible, and suggesting alternatives is crucial. Maintaining a balance ensures that requests align with showcasing the PoC, advancing success criteria, and avoiding delays.

## Don't Assume!

Eliminate assumptions and ambiguous, or loosely defined statements. Clarity and specificity are vital in each document section. Engage in self-editing, and seek external review, preferably from someone familiar with the solution but not directly involved. This approach ensures document clarity and completeness.

## Engage Your Manager

Incorporate your sales engineering manager in reviewing and providing input on the PoC strategy. This collaborative approach not only ensures a high-quality PoC document but also serves as an opportunity for coaching and support, fostering trust and engagement.

The SE leading a PoC should inform and engage their manager in a timely and collaborative manner. Since they are not mired in the details they can serve as a sounding board for you. Their experience and perspective can serve you well to avoid common blind spots and pitfalls.

## Know Where the Finish Line Is

Always be aware of the finish line for a PoC. Clearly define when adequate progress has been made to illustrate the solution's value. This documented finish line is essential for both the sales team and the customer, preventing unnecessary time expenditure on the PoC without reaching a decisive outcome.

# Outcomes

The **Define** milestone culminates in a completed PoC Agreement document, reflecting how you and the customer will manage the PoC. This document encompasses the business context, success metrics, roles and responsibilities, and the PoCs conclusion. Collaborative efforts, iterations, and careful completion of each section ensure a polished and professional document ready for customer review.

By adhering to these guidelines and embracing a collaborative, balanced approach, you pave the way for a successful Define milestone, setting the stage for a seamless transition into the **Execute** milestone.

# 9

# Milestone 03 | EXECUTE

## Overview

The purpose of the **Execute** milestone is to successfully finalize the Proof of Concept outlined in the PoC Agreement Template document. The ultimate objective of this milestone is to secure a positive technical decision from the customer.

During the **Execute** milestone, the sales engineer takes a leading role in coordinating the PoC. The account executive continues involvement, particularly in addressing any process or engagement issues that may arise with the customer.

## Focus

The primary focus of the **Execute** milestone is for the sales engineer to actively contribute to the completion of the PoC. This crucial phase demands a collaborative approach, emphasizing high-quality and professional customer engagement.

Throughout this milestone, the sales engineer showcases both technical expertise and diplomatic skills. Given the inevitable challenges that arise during a PoC, regular check-ins with the sales team are essential to stay on course. In times of issues, a cohesive team effort is crucial for resolution.

```
Note to account executives: during this milestone, it is crucial
to support your sales engineer by refraining from introducing
additional tasks to the PoC, especially in the customer's presence.
```

This not only disrespects the agreed-upon PoC Agreement but also opens the door for customer requests that may complicate matters. *Avoid putting the sales engineer in a difficult position and introducing unnecessary risks to the PoC.*

During the **Execute** milestone, the clock begins ticking for the PoC timeline. Adhering to the what, when, where, who, and how is vital once the clock starts. This PoC timeline resembles the countdown clock seen in movies, though our goal is not as dramatic – it's the countdown to completing the PoC and securing the technical win.

To achieve this, maintaining focus and managing the time required for PoC completion is crucial. This is driven by the sales team's need to wrap up the PoC within a timeframe conducive to winning the opportunity. Additionally, ensuring customer engagement amid their other projects and responsibilities is paramount.

I firmly believe in short engagements to sustain enthusiasm for the PoC.

Stick to the plan and only consider adjustments after thorough discussions with the entire team. Specifically, refrain from making decisions unilaterally – collaboration is key.

From a practical standpoint, this means refraining from making additions or removals from the PoC without comprehensive internal discussions. Numerous changes or decisions made without careful thought and coordination can disrupt the meticulous planning invested up to this point.

## Best Practices

In the pursuit of successful execution during this critical milestone, consider these best practices.

First, *adhere strictly to the defined scope of the Proof of Concept (PoC) as articulated in the PoC Agreement document.* Resist the temptation to augment this agreement without consulting the sales team extensively, and gauging the potential impact on the PoC. A comprehensive understanding of the ramifications of introducing new elements is vital, particularly to their effects on the timing and overall success of the PoC.

Second, *maintain an open and consistent dialogue as a sales engineer.* Resist the urge to retreat to familiar technological ground. Actively engage in discussions, seeking feedback from the customer. A consistent communication cadence not only fosters progress and better adoption but also contributes to building a strong working relationship.

Third, *be proactive in escalating issues early if specific events, tasks, resources, or timelines appear challenging to meet.* Safeguard against delays that could jeopardize the completion of your PoC. Rather than attempting to solve every issue independently, collaborate with fellow sales engineers, managers, and other experts within the organization. Seeking input from others showcases the attributes of a well-rounded and confident sales engineer.

Even with meticulous planning, challenges may arise during a PoC. Preparation equips the PoC team to navigate these challenges effectively. The essence of overcoming these hurdles lies in acknowledging their existence, coupled with the necessary training and mindset to address them as efficiently as possible.

Now, let's consider the outcomes tied to the **Execute** milestone, with a focus on three indicators of success:

1. **Complete the PoC:** Regularly review and update the PoC Agreement Template document. These updates should encompass comments, experiences, and the results of testing against success criteria, as well as customer feedback. Documenting these updates is crucial for readiness in the PoC Key Findings Meeting during the **Close** milestone.

2. **Validate the Success Criteria:** Ensure completion of all success criteria items listed in the PoC document. If a specific item proves challenging, document it. Your objective is to position yourself to showcase the best possible outcome of the PoC in the subsequent Close milestone.

3. **Plan for Success in the PoC Key Findings Meeting:** Recognize that the actions taken in the **Execute** milestone will significantly influence the success of the upcoming PoC Key Findings Meeting. Executing the PoC is only one aspect; equally important is collecting substantial evidence of its success. As the lead sales engineer, avoid reliance on memory; instead, meticulously capture the process, conversations, and results, regardless of their nature. This practice ensures control during the PoC Key Findings Meeting, providing documented proof of success and countering any opposing perspectives.

With the completion of these steps, the PoC concludes, and it is time to transition to the **Close** Milestone.

# 10

# Milestone 04 | CLOSE

## Overview

In the pursuit of a successful **Close** milestone, it's essential to begin by updating the PoC Agreement Template document to accurately reflect the proceedings of the **Execute** Milestone.

*There is an art to executing a world-class Proof of Concept, some of that art is the essential need to foster a strong relationship with the customer, your solution, and organization.*

The management of this relationship commences in the early stages of the **Qualify** milestone and evolves throughout the **Define** and **Execute** milestones.

    However, it's often in the Close milestone that this crucial
    relationship aspect is overlooked and forgotten.

Regrettably, I observe that the **Close** milestone is frequently mishandled by most sales teams. Recognizing the significance of this issue, the **Close** Milestone stands out as the most pivotal among the four milestones, particularly considering the emphasis on relationship-building.

With a few strategic adjustments, the **Close** milestone can be harnessed to guarantee an energetic conclusion that culminates the efforts invested in the preceding three milestones. It is imperative to approach this milestone with the same level of focus, energy, and momentum as the other milestones to fully capitalize on the achievements of the PoC. This is where you not only sell but also market the efforts and results from the **Execute** milestone.

Completing the documented requirements of the PoC does not signify victory. Even if your PoC stakeholders express excitement about the results, winning or acquiring a purchase order is not guaranteed. The actual work of securing a technical win and obtaining the purchase order unfolds in the **Close** milestone. This stage grants you access to decision-makers who play a pivotal role in confirming the technical win and discussing the purchase order.

Even after completing the technical aspects in the **Execute** milestone, you are still actively selling your solution during the **Close** milestone. The success or failure in this phase significantly influences your chances of securing a purchase order.

Focus is crucial in this milestone, which aims to bring the PoC to completion, allowing the sales team to present successful results to customer stakeholders. This presentation occurs through the PoC Key Findings Meeting, where the outcomes are displayed and explained to showcase the success of your solution.

The **Close** milestone signifies a shift from a "Proof" to a "Purchase," transitioning the PoC from a "technical" to a "business" focus and engagement. The PoC Key Findings Meeting becomes instrumental in aligning the politics and processes within the customer's organization to garner support and approval for a technical win. Achieving a technical win paves the way for discussions on terms and conditions.

While this milestone involves the entire sales team, the account executive takes center stage, responsible for scheduling the PoC Key Findings Meeting.

The sales engineer remains engaged, collaborating with the account executive to summarize and translate PoC outcomes into a compelling sales pitch.

A crucial shift in perspective occurs during this milestone regarding the results and outcomes of the PoC in the **Execute** milestone. It is vital to translate the technical experience into business benefits, with an emphasis on making the conversation 80% business-focused and 20% technology-focused. This percentage is more of a guideline to encourage the sales team to shift towards a business mindset rather than being fixated on technical details. While technical qualities are essential, framing them in a business context as benefits to the customer is paramount.

> *The value of the PoC Key Findings Meeting lies in providing customer stakeholders with a concise, business-focused summary of the PoC and how the solution addresses their requirements positively.*

Executing a compelling **Close** milestone extends the perceived value of the PoC, allowing you to amplify your solution's impact in various ways:

- Emphasize how you met or exceeded PoC objectives and success metrics.
- Provide a platform to broadcast PoC results to critical customer stakeholders beyond the core PoC team.
- Gather support and clarification of the PoC with a focus on business benefits, as nobody buys a solution without clear and measurable benefits.
- Confirm with the customer regarding the impact, experiences, and results experienced in the PoC.
- Actively sell the effects and benefits to drive a decision in favor of your solution, taking ownership of ensuring your solution is front and center with the customer.

Closing a PoC is a blend of art and science, demanding a thoughtful approach. It is crucial to halt customer access to the PoC environment once success criteria have been met, steering clear of the temptation to extend with a "one more thing" scenario.

# The A-B-C Framework

To manage this effectively, ensure that the PoC environment is inaccessible. Closing a PoC involves tailored steps based on the nature of the solution. Employ the A-B-C framework to craft specific actions and processes for a seamless conclusion.

## Affirm

Affirm business objectives, success metrics, and outcomes by capturing the PoC experience. Track progress at each milestone, packaging findings in a compelling narrative rather than mere facts and figures. Rally support from key stakeholders; don't presume unanimous agreement—seek and confirm their backing.

## Broadcast

Conduct individual and group sessions to review and discuss PoC results. Articulate achievements, both expected and unexpected, diplomatically and persistently. Broadcast the success of the PoC to other stakeholders.

## Cleanup

Thoroughly document to create an accurate PoC history, tying up any loose ends or tasks. Disable access to software, documentation, artifacts, and hardware related to the PoC, including customer access to SaaS environments in the cloud.

## Markers of a Successful Close

Ensure the following *markers of success* are apparent when closing a PoC, serving as a dashboard for performance feedback:

- **Agreed-To Close Date**: establish a clear endpoint for the PoC. Refuse to keep it open once success criteria are met.
- **Internal Sales Team Pre-Close Meeting**: assess PoC achievements as a sales team, preparing for the subsequent PoC Key Findings Meeting.
- **Core Customer PoC Team Pre-Meeting**: address outstanding issues with the core customer team before formal meetings with key stakeholders.

For sure there are many more markers of success in closing a PoC. However, I found during my tenure that the most notable trap is *not setting the expectation of what occurs after a PoC is closed.*

The focus of these markers is all about ensuring you have clearly defined and agreed-to next steps. Failure to have these defined during the **Define** milestone results in placing your next sales stage in jeopardy.

This concludes the **Close** milestone. At this point, the focus moves from the sales engineer to the account executive - meaning it moves from a technical focus to a sales focus.

# III

# The Essential Template

*When undertaking a journey you need to ensure you have proper equipment and travel gear.*

*Whether it's a map, compass, or GPS device knowing what to take and how to use it ensures you complete your journey.*

# 11

# The PoC Agreement Template

E mbarking on a Proof of Concept mirrors a project, demanding a robust framework and methodology for optimal execution. Up to this point, our focus has been on dissecting the framework and methods crucial for successful Proof of Concept implementation.

Now, let's delve into the key template essential for crafting a *Statement of Work* for a Proof of Concept - which we refer to as the PoC Agreement Template. This tool is instrumental for sales engineers as they navigate the process.

The PoC Agreement Template comprises several sections, each serving a distinct purpose to ensure comprehensive coverage of business, technology, and process considerations during the Proof of Concept. Each section builds on the other and are by nature interconnected as they progressively provide clarity on the what, who, when, and how of a PoC.

It is crucial to recognize that this PoC Agreement is designed for swift and effective information capture. Its purpose is to equip sales engineers with a comprehensive statement of work, delineating the necessary PoC elements essential for achieving a technical victory.

I present this template as a foundational framework for the global sales engineering community. Essentially, it functions as a collaborative effort, drawing upon the collective insights of contributors.

*By sharing this version, I aim to invite constructive feedback, intending to refine and enhance the template further.*

The focus of this chapter is to look at each of the sections of the PoC Agreement Template. Each section is not only explained in terms of its objective but is also accompanied by best practices to ensure the inclusion of the right content.

The PoC Agreement Template consists of the following sections:

- Purpose of the Document
- Current State
- Future State
- Business Imperatives
- The Gap
- Outcomes
- Proposed Solution
- Scope
- Success Criteria
- Technical Requirements
- Supplemental Documentation
- Assumptions
- Timeline
- Roles and Responsibilities
- Sequence of Events
- Path to Procurement
- Closure
- Acknowledgment

# Purpose of the Document

## Objective

This section is an overall high-level general outline regarding what this PoC Agreement contains relative to your customer.

## Best Practices

This section requires little or no change from one customer to another other than to insert your *company name,* the *name of the customer,* and the signatures of the account executive and sales engineer who are executing this PoC.

# Current State

## Objective

This section describes the customer's prevailing situation from a business and operational perspective.

## Best Practices

In the journey of understanding our customers, it is paramount to have them articulate their present circumstances. This revelation serves as a profound glimpse into their daily challenges. Utilize this comprehension as the compass guiding the alignment of their envisioned future and the solution that will aptly cater to their needs.

Exercise caution when dealing with customers who provide scant details about their current situation. This is an opportune moment to attentively listen and meticulously document the nuances of the customer's experience. This insight becomes a treasure trove later on, as you endeavor to elucidate how your proposed solution seamlessly addresses their existing challenges and propels them towards a more favorable future state.

This stage is pivotal for capturing the authentic "voice of the customer" and understanding their predicament in their own words. Encouraging customers to independently articulate their situation is a best practice. This may seem inconsequential, but it stands as a vital contribution from the customer. Since they are the ones immersed in their current reality, they are best equipped to articulate the nuances of their circumstances. Requesting customers to compose this narrative is consistently well-received, as it actively involves them in the Proof of Concept (PoC) process.

It's essential to guide customers in ensuring that their descriptions focus on the business aspects rather than delving into technical intricacies. At this juncture, a technical discourse is unnecessary. The emphasis should be on understanding the business landscape of their current state. This business-centric focus facilitates a profound comprehension of what instigated the need for a PoC.

A crucial piece of advice is to refrain from relying on marketing materials to shape the content of this section. The narrative should invariably emerge from the customer's own words. A sales engineer should exercise prudence in avoiding the imposition of external perspectives, allowing the customer's authentic voice to resonate throughout.

## Future State

### Objective

This section describes the customer's expected future aspirations or requirements from a business and operational perspective.

## Best Practices

Encouraging customers to articulate their vision for the future provides valuable insights into the necessary changes based on their current experiences. In the Future State section, it is crucial to elicit descriptions that may be either factual or aspirational. The key is to have customers articulate their envisioned future environment using their own words. We are not seeking definitive descriptions at this stage; instead, the focus is on capturing the customer's perspective.

From the standpoint of a solution vendor, it is imperative to allow customers the freedom to be either concise or verbose in expressing their aspirations. I have observed instances where customers provide brief sentences or detailed narratives envisioning a future state where everything seamlessly works together. The length or detail of the description is inconsequential; what matters is that it is conveyed in the customer's authentic voice.

This section is dedicated to understanding the changes customers desire from their perspective. However, it's essential to note that, as a sales team, there is no obligation or expectation to materialize this future state during the Proof of Concept (PoC) engagement.

Similar to the Current State section, the emphasis in the Future State section remains on the business aspect rather than the technological intricacies. Often, customers may not take the time to contemplate the future, especially from a business standpoint. Thus, guiding them through this exercise serves as a valuable opportunity to reshape their understanding of an improved solution.

Both the Current and Future State sections serve as crucial frameworks for evaluating the success of a PoC during the PoC Key Findings Meeting.

# Business Imperatives

## Objective

This section identifies the customer's Business Imperatives as it relates to their requirements to improve their current state.

## Best Practices

It is crucial to confine the business imperatives within the parameters of the Proof of Concept (PoC). Customers may sometimes extend their considerations beyond the illustrative nature of the PoC, veering into an implementation perspective prematurely. Although a sales engineer might be eager to delve into technical details in this section, it's advisable to resist that inclination, as subsequent sections are designated for collecting such specifics.

Emphasize business-centric statements and comprehend the business implications before delving into the technological facets of the PoC. The initial sections underscore a deliberate focus on business rather than technology. This intentional design aims to maintain equilibrium between these two aspects.

Similar to the Current and Future States, the customer is encouraged to articulate this section in their own words. Nevertheless, in this phase, the sales team can offer guidance and support since the customer requesting the PoC may not always consider the broader scope and impact.

A valuable strategy is to request that someone a level or two above the primary PoC contact contribute to this section. This approach ensures a more comprehensive perspective while also making certain that the contributor is well-versed in the intricacies of the PoC. Subsequently, this individual can be leveraged as an executive or VITO (Very Important Top Officer) level contact.

# The Gap

## Objective

In this section, have the customer list what is currently missing from a business and operational perspective.

## Best Practices

Inquiring with the customer about current limitations in their environment serves as a means to discern and qualify success criteria, as later expounded upon in this document. The identified gaps may pertain to either business or technology.

The effectiveness of the Gap list is heightened when it is compiled by the customer. It is imperative to guarantee the comprehensiveness and accuracy of this list. For optimal clarity, I recommend presenting the gap items in a succinct bullet-point format, emphasizing brief, descriptive points rather than elaborate explanations in this section.

# Outcomes

## Objective

In this section, the required Outcomes of the PoC span, both tactical or experiential outcomes.

## Best Practices

In contrast to earlier sections, the Outcomes segment is predominantly crafted by a sales engineer. Within this section, a comprehensive business overview unfolds, illustrating how your suggested solution harmonizes with the Current State.

It is imperative to articulate Outcomes that are distinctly defined within the context of this Proof of Concept (PoC), focusing on the specific needs rather than the overall capabilities of the proposed solution. This portion should, to a certain extent, delve into both the present and future states while addressing the customer's Business Imperatives. Moreover, it is crucial to highlight how you intend to address and resolve some, or all, of the identified gaps.

Adhering to best practices, it is recommended to curate a concise list of outcomes, emphasizing quality over quantity. The aim is to present a succinct and impactful representation rather than an exhaustive enumeration.

# Proposed Solution

## Objective

In this section, you will describe the proposed solution that will be used in the PoC.

## Best Practices

In crafting the Proposed Solution section, the sales engineer is encouraged to leverage pre-existing, concise boilerplate descriptions readily accessible from our product marketing site. The general rule is to employ standardized content unless there's a specific element of the solution that is either unnecessary or requires exclusion. Maintaining brevity is crucial; our goal is to confine this section to a single page whenever feasible.

The emphasis within this segment should be on a marketing-oriented approach, as opposed to delving into an exhaustive technical or architectural overview.

If additional supporting documents with more in-depth information are deemed necessary, it is recommended to incorporate links rather than bloating the PoC document with excessive marketing and supporting details. This approach ensures a streamlined and focused presentation.

# Scope

## Objective

In this section, you will define the scope of the PoC by establishing a limited set of clearly defined and measurable goals.

## Best Practices

Before delving into the detailed success criteria, it's essential to establish the boundaries of the Proof of Concept (PoC) scope. Considering the capabilities of your solution, it's crucial to define what aspects of the customer's requirements and your solution's overall capabilities will be demonstrated through this PoC.

This practice fosters a shared understanding between you and the customer, effectively preventing scope creep in the future. When crafting the Scope section, adhere to several best practices, including:

- Clearly articulating that the PoC environment is temporary and should not be utilized as a production environment.
- Emphasizing that any activities conducted during the PoC should not be employed for staging or setting up a pre-production environment.
- Enumerating all expectations regarding the PoC scope. It's advisable to err on the side of inclusivity, listing every detail to avoid making assumptions later.

It is imperative that these points are thoroughly discussed and comprehended by all parties involved. This approach aligns with the principles of effective communication and clarity, promoting a successful and mutually beneficial PoC experience.

# Success Criteria

## Objective

This section will capture the items that define the primary success of the PoC. These criteria provide evidence of how your solution meets your customer's requirements.

## Best Practices

In the preceding sections, we delved into the business aspect of our discussion. Now, let's shift our focus away from the business lens and delve into the technical intricacies of demonstrating the value of your solution to the customer.

The Success Criteria stands as the compass guiding the actions of the sales engineer. Think of it as a scoring grid, determining the degree of success in meeting customer expectations. In simple terms, excelling in each success criterion is pivotal for securing victory in the Proof of Concept (PoC).

This section, akin to the heart of the PoC document, sets the finish line for the entire endeavor. Picture it as participating in a hurdles race, where not only must you traverse a track but also surmount a series of hurdles. Success criteria act as these hurdles – to reach the finish line, you must navigate both running and leaping over a series of obstacles.

For a sales engineer, the ability to define success criteria becomes the linchpin, influencing the complexity and success of the PoC. Let's explore some best practices for identifying and managing success criteria:

- Relevance Matters: Only include success criteria addressable by the proposed solution within the context and scope of the PoC.
- Clarity is Key: Articulate and define each success criterion, avoiding general statements or requirements.
- Paint the Picture of Success: Describe what success looks like for each criterion to ensure alignment between you and the customer on the desired outcome.
- Limit and Focus: Keep the number of success criteria reasonable. PoCs aren't about testing every feature; rather, they're focused on key aspects.
- Contextual Connection: Ensure each success criterion relates to the Current, Future, Gap, and Outcomes sections.
- Showcase Differentiation: Include criteria highlighting your competitive edge.

Moving into the Execute milestone, having well-defined success criteria becomes your map for navigating the PoC. Regular updates to this section serve as a real-time indicator of the PoCs progress and proximity to completion.

Feedback from sales engineers emphasizes the importance of maintaining this section. Keep a "scoring sheet" documenting completion status, results, outcomes, comments, and experiences related to each criterion. This information proves invaluable during the PoC Key Findings Meeting in the Close milestone.

Closing the PoC hinges on correctly managing the Success Criteria section. Failure to control this aspect can result in ongoing customer requests, prolonging the PoC and potentially jeopardizing overall success.

Crafting the Success Criteria falls squarely on the shoulders of the sales engineer. While the sales engineer owns this section, customer input is crucial, making it a mutually defined and agreed-upon aspect.

An indispensable element is the inclusion of competitive differentiators. As the lead sales engineer, taking charge of and managing this section is paramount to ward off competition.

Striking a balance between customer needs and illustrating what should be showcased in the PoC demands a collaborative approach. The success criteria act as your compass, guiding you through the PoC journey to its successful conclusion.

Ensuring well-defined, achievable success criteria that showcase the best of your solution is pivotal for securing the technical win. To boost your success rate, prioritize clear and measurable success criteria.

# Technical Requirements

## Objective

In this section, list the Technical Requirements needed to enable the setup and execution of the PoC environment.

## Best Practices

It is the sales engineer who takes charge of completing this section to pinpoint any necessary prerequisites essential for accessing the PoC environment.

This free-format section serves as a repository for all pertinent technical details crucial for implementing the solution from a technical standpoint. Successful completion of this section hinges on effective collaboration with the customer to ascertain the feasibility of meeting these technical requirements in terms of physical setup, security access, and timing. Clear communication and mutual understanding in these areas pave the way for a timely commencement of the PoC.

An overarching principle guiding this process is to refrain from requesting items that do not align with the overall capabilities of your solution. Maintaining focus on essentials not only streamlines the process but also ensures the customer can promptly facilitate the required items.

# Supplemental Documentation

## Objective

In this section, you will capture other related and instructive information that supports or clarifies the PoC.

## Best Practices

In this segment, it's crucial to incorporate references to other relevant and informative materials that can enlighten the customer about the proposed solution. Customers often seek additional resources, whether in marketing, training, or technical aspects, to gain a deeper understanding.

By furnishing links to these documents, you empower the customer to delve into the intricacies of your solution. However, exercise caution in your selection; avoid including information that may cause unease or lead them down irrelevant paths.

We recommend employing a concise bulleted list with embedded links rather than inserting separate documents. This approach ensures the document remains manageable in size.

Remember, this section is not obligatory but can be leveraged strategically. Be intentional about the information you present, adhering to the principle of "less is more." Prioritize items that both inform and instruct the customer, fostering their confidence in the solution. Embrace the wisdom of "less is more" as you curate a list that enhances their understanding and trust.

# Assumptions

## Objective

This section documents all customer and solution vendor assumptions of the PoC.

## Best Practices

In the pursuit of a successful Proof of Concept (PoC), it is imperative to gather and clarify assumptions from both the customer and the solution vendor. Assumptions encompass a wide range of details, from task assignments and the choice of pencil color for grading sheets to responsibilities like fetching coffee. Naturally, this also extends to what tasks will be accomplished and their respective timelines.

The underlying principle is to be thorough in considering anything that could potentially disrupt or hinder the success of the PoC. Failing to capture these assumptions may have repercussions later in the PoC process. From my own experiences, I've observed that these assumptions wield significant influence over the PoCs scope and trajectory.

Recognize that success lies in the meticulous attention given to details and assumptions, ensuring a solid foundation for the Proof of Concept journey.

# Timeline

## Objective

In this section, clearly define the timeline in which the PoC will be executed.

## Best Practices

To successfully execute a Proof of Concept (PoC) within a specified timeframe, it is essential to adopt a project management mindset. One common cause for a PoC veering off course can be attributed to the absence of a project management approach.

I acknowledge that many sales engineers, myself included, may not have formal training in project management processes and practices. However, grasping the fundamentals is relatively straightforward. While I don't insist that sales engineers undergo an exhaustive project management course, acquiring an understanding of the principles governing effective people and process management can significantly enhance performance. Even a basic comprehension of these principles can bring value and streamline the execution of a PoC.

Every PoC operates within constraints of time, resources, and access to individuals. Applying a project management mindset is instrumental in preventing scope creep. Furthermore, executing a PoC proficiently not only optimizes resources but also presents a polished and professional image of your organization to the customer.

Establishing a clear timeline is crucial for orchestrating the right events and ensuring that the right individuals are synchronized at the appropriate moments to propel the PoC forward.

Another pivotal aspect of PoC management involves judicious allocation of time. It is customary to inquire about the desired duration from the customer, but it is advisable to steer away from this practice. Instead, the sales engineer should guide the customer on a realistic completion timeline rather than accepting a protracted timeframe based solely on customer preferences. Discrepancies between the customer's expectations and the actual time required are not uncommon. While customer input is valued, it is the responsibility of the project manager to recommend a more suitable timeframe.

As a sales engineer, you wield influence over the completion timeline of a PoC. Therefore, it is imperative to align the ability to finalize the PoC with the broader sales strategy, ensuring it complements the optimal window for closing the associated opportunity.

# Roles and Responsibilities

## Objective

In this section, list the roles and responsibilities of the active participants and stakeholders in the PoC.

## Best Practices

Ensuring effective engagement in a Proof of Concept (PoC) begins with a clear identification of key stakeholders. This step is crucial for focused follow-ups and sustained involvement throughout the PoC process. It involves identifying all stakeholders, participants, and interested parties associated with the PoC.

While this may seem like an administrative task, it is a vital aspect of the PoC journey. Proper completion requires specific details such as names, titles, roles, and contact information. The PoC Agreement Template provides standardized naming conventions, adaptable to your industry.

Although often perceived as bureaucratic, this section is a critical compilation of individuals who should be informed and actively participate in the PoC.

To ensure the right customer stakeholders are engaged, it's essential to categorize and involve representatives from four key groups:

1. **Executives**: These leaders confirm the PoCs necessity, ensuring allocated resources align with budgetary considerations, access to funding, solution requirements, and commitment from their teams.
2. **Middle Managers**: As vital enablers, middle managers stay informed about the PoC, ensuring the appropriate team members remain engaged.
3. **Customer Participants**: These individuals play an active role in testing, validating, advising, and participating in the PoC.
4. **Decision Makers**: This category includes individuals responsible for decision approvals and, crucially, those involved in the purchasing process. Including purchasing contacts and defining a "path to purchase" is essential to clarify and qualify the customer's intent to engage in a PoC.

It's imperative to identify individuals within each category along with their contact information. This not only facilitates document sharing but also allows for effective follow-ups with key stakeholders, preventing reliance on a single contact or gatekeeper.

A red flag should be raised if, during this process, only one person is identified across various roles. This suggests a potential lack of access to executives or insufficient support for the PoC.

This section gains even more significance when preparing for the PoC Key Findings Meeting, serving as a comprehensive directory for inviting essential participants to this critical gathering.

## Sequence of Events

### Objective

In this section, identify the timelines and critical milestones of specific events to ensure the right actions, meetings, and activities necessary to complete the PoC.

## Best Practices

To effectively manage the Proof of Concept (PoC) process, it is crucial to maintain a comprehensive list of events. This list should outline the necessary steps in a clear and well-understood sequence. Such clarity ensures that both the customer and the sales team have a distinct understanding of the actions that need to take place, the timing of these events, and the individuals involved.

Various methods exist for defining and managing this list, ranging from a straightforward bulleted format to the use of a comprehensive project management application. Regardless of the chosen approach, the key is to have a well-defined list in place.

My recommendation is to start with a basic milestone-driven list. As the PoC progresses and becomes more defined, allow the level of detail to expand over time. Many successful sales engineers follow the principle of "less is more" in the initial stages of PoC discussions to prevent overwhelming the customer. Once we make progress in delineating the PoC, additional steps can be incorporated as needed.

The Sequence of Events is pivotal in establishing the necessary steps to complete a PoC within the designated timeline. This strategic approach, guided by a well-organized event sequence, ensures a smooth and efficient PoC process.

# Path to Procurement

## Objective

In this section, list the people, steps, timelines, assumptions and requirements of how a solution will be purchased once a customer selects a solution from the PoC.

## Best Practices

In the pursuit of a successful solution acquisition post Proof of Concept (PoC), this crucial section holds immense significance. Its purpose is to discern and qualify the intent and desire of the customer with the emphasis in this section focused on:

- Unveiling the intricacies of the procurement process in collaboration with the customer.
- Expanding our awareness to individuals integral to the purchasing journey, extending beyond the stakeholders directly engaged in the PoC.
- Gaining insights into the requisite steps, timelines, and signatures is indispensable for sealing the deal.

This segment must be diligently handled by the account executive rather than the sales engineer. A savvy sales team must grasp the procurement pathway before committing to a Proof of Concept.

The failure of the sales team to capture this vital information or a customer's reluctance to share such details should serve as warning signals. They suggest potential hurdles that may impede the successful culmination of the purchase.

# Closure

## Objective

This section defines when and how a PoC ends - specifically how the PoC environment, processes, and team wind down.

## Best Practices

Beginning a Proof of Concept effectively is crucial, but equally significant is knowing when and how to conclude it. A well-thought-out closure plan not only communicates to the customer that the PoC is not indefinite but also signals a decisive point of decision-making.

Outlining the steps in advance is key to managing expectations and ensuring a PoC concludes at a predefined juncture. This defined closure is not only beneficial for you as a solution vendor but also serves as a clear indication to the customer that a pivotal moment has arrived. Valuable resources cannot be indefinitely allocated, and having a planned closure allows for a strategic shift.

Moreover, a structured closure plan facilitates transitioning into the opportunity-closing phase with the customer. The PoC Key Findings Meeting becomes the catalyst for action, wherein the account executive actively seeks business engagement. To ensure a smooth process, consider the following best practices:

- Schedule the PoC Key Findings Meeting, specifying the date and location, with the PoC stakeholders.
- Allocate sufficient time for your internal sales team to prepare adequately for the meeting. A prompt and professional presentation is key.
- Confirm with the customer that the Success Criteria have been met.
- Before the meeting, address any lingering concerns raised by the customer.
- Clearly outline the removal or shutdown of any PoC-related assets and determine who will be responsible and when this action will occur.
- Summarize the meeting outcomes in an email to the customer, providing final closure to the PoC.

By proactively sharing this information with customers in advance, you ensure they understand that a PoC has a defined and purposeful endpoint. This clarity is essential for effective collaboration and decision-making.

## Acknowledgment

### Objective

This section is a non-binding, non-legal section that acknowledges the nature of this PoC. It also allows for physical or electronic signatures.

### Best Practices

This marks the concluding segment of the Proof of Concept (PoC) Agreement Template, serving as a non-binding and clear-cut signature page, devoid of legal complexities.

Should a customer encounter challenges in signing, it is unnecessary to escalate the matter. Various circumstances may prevent a customer from signing a document. Instead, kindly request the customer's acknowledgment of the PoC Agreement using an email, including the attached PoC Agreement document.

## Get Your Copy of the PoC Agreement Template

For a downloadable version of this template refer to the Final Comments and Resources section. this book.

# IV

# Essential Realities

*Like any journey, expect moments of drama and potential danger. Be aware of possible challenges even as you plan effectively.*

*Knowing the potential pitfalls and common issues faced while on your PoC journey will help you navigate and manage it with a world-class stride.*

# 12

# Leading Practices of a World-Class PoC

I n this chapter, I aim to present a concise set of practices to ensure the successful navigation of your Proof of Concept. While each practice could merit its own chapter, I intend to keep these guidelines brief yet impactful. These bite-sized insights aim to guide you through the best practices essential for mastering the dynamics of a world-class PoC.

## Have a Customer Lens

In the pursuit of success, it's evident that having the "best technology" doesn't always guarantee victory. Despite possessing a superior solution, we often find ourselves overlooked by customers.

The key lies in comprehending our customers better, a crucial factor that goes beyond technological prowess. To truly succeed, we must adopt the perspective of our customers when navigating the Proof of Concept.

This means investing the time to grasp the reality faced by our customers. A significant aspect of this reality is their desire to advance and secure their careers. Consequently, decisions are made to steer clear of personal or reputational risks.

IBM's savvy marketing encapsulates this concept with their phrase, "no one ever gets fired for buying IBM." This approach allowed customers to choose IBM, not necessarily for its cutting-edge technology, but due to the reduced risk associated with the brand. Establishing an impression that minimizes the risk of opting for a particular solution, whether grounded in reality or perception, can be a game-changer.

In the PoC journey, the focus should be on diminishing the customer's perception of risk. This involves demonstrating genuine care and concern for the customer and posing questions that delve into their aspirations and challenges. Some questions to ask include; Is this PoC a stepping stone to a larger project? Could success in the PoC lead to a promotion or demotion? What are the political dynamics influencing the selection process? Which executives hold a vested interest in the PoC outcome?

*Embrace curiosity about your customer beyond technical specifications.*

Understand the dynamics surrounding them. Elevate your customer during the PoC, ensuring their association with you and your solution is perceived as beneficial. The aim is to eliminate any apprehension, making it an easy decision for them to choose you, even if the "best technology" is not on your side.

In essence, building authentic relationships is the cornerstone of delivering a high-quality customer experience throughout the PoC journey. Adopting this approach not only acknowledges the importance of understanding the customer but also actively working towards making them look great during the process.

# Having a Sales Strategy is Essential!

A clear and articulated account sales strategy is indispensable when considering a PoC. Your PoC should align with your overall account sales strategy, much like a travel bucket list identifies preferred locations and experiences. An account plan, akin to your bucket list, outlines the people, places, and solutions you aim to engage with your customers.

Before delving into a PoC, ensure your account sales strategy is documented. This safeguards against pursuing a PoC that deviates from your account plan. While no plan is flawless, adjustments within the context of an account sales strategy are acceptable and even necessary.

# Adopt Common-Sense Sales Practices

During a PoC, adhere to common-sense sales practices. Building relationships, understanding budget processes, timing, access to decision-makers, and comprehending customer requirements remain crucial.

Leverage time-tested sales engineering practices throughout the qualifying, documenting, executing, and closing milestones. Consistent and thoughtful practices during a PoC display your team, solution, and culture at their best.

# Avoid Getting Cornered

Sales engineers often have stories of accepting PoCs they shouldn't have, usually due to pressure from customers, account executives, or internal decisions. While getting cornered can happen to the best of us, recognizing the situation and seeking an early exit can earn respect.

Incorporate built-in exit points during the Qualify & Document milestones of your PoC engagement. Some may argue against backing out, but I contend it's possible and sometimes necessary. Explain to customers why a PoC isn't required, accompanied by a clear communication strategy and an alternative plan to address their requests or requirements.

Walking back a PoC with transparency and diplomacy, though challenging, outweighs the downside of continuing with an ill-advised PoC.

## Ensure You Solve Real Problems

Understand the problem you're solving for the customer before committing to a PoC. A PoC is about addressing a business issue, not just showcasing technical capabilities. Define the problem's nature, impact, frequency, and affected parties to ensure the sales team focuses on the business side rather than solely on technical aspects.

Identifying a business issue in a PoC is critical; otherwise, it may become a mere research project or tire-kicking exercise. Collaborate with customers who are transparent about their needs, budget, access to decision-makers, and time frames. Proceed cautiously if any of these elements are missing.

## Clarify the Purpose ("P" for Purpose)

Before delving deep into a PoC, understand its purpose. While the "P" in PoC stands for proof, it can also signify *purpose*—the reason for undertaking the effort. A PoC serves various purposes, one being to shape the customer's perception of your solution.

Avoid using a PoC as an educational tool for the customer, as it can be expensive and rarely leads to a purchase. Instead, employ alternative, less costly approaches for educating customers, such as white papers, videos, one-on-one sessions with a sales engineer, customer references, and success stories.

## Plan and Execute with Precision

Approach a PoC with a project management mindset by creating a defined statement of work. Proper planning and execution, along with a PoC Agreement Template, contribute to a smoother process. This serves as the *statement of work*. I suggest having this statement of work is non-negotiable and essential for engaging with customers properly and professionally.

When facing resistance to creating a statement of work, proceed with caution, as it may indicate the customer's unwillingness or inability to participate effectively. Be vigilant, and have an exit strategy if necessary.

## Set Clear Boundaries

Know when to say no to certain requests within a PoC. Communicate this clearly and quickly to your account executive, offering alternative approaches when declining. While customer requests during a PoC are typically not malicious, setting boundaries and explaining your rationale is crucial.

Evaluate new requests based on their impact on PoC objectives and timelines. Strike a balance between being open to considerations and maintaining boundaries to ensure a successful and timely PoC.

## Maintain Open and Transparent Communication

As the leader of the PoC, the sales engineer must uphold consistent communication. Regular updates using various mediums, such as meetings, electronic communication, voice, and video, are essential. Voice-to-voice updates followed by written summaries are preferable for maintaining a strong broadcasting signal.

Regardless of the communication medium, ensure updates are concise, actionable, and timely. Consistent communication is key to keeping the PoC on track.

## Maintain Thorough and Complete Documentation

Documenting every aspect of your PoC is crucial. Consistent documentation as you progress reduces the time, effort, and stress associated with recalling and recording information later. Failure to document can influence the direction and progress of your PoC negatively.

Adhering to a disciplined documentation approach showcases your professionalism and helps you remain in control of your PoC.

## Manage Requests and Scope-Creep

Once the PoC Agreement is complete, avoid changes to prevent scope-creep. When changes are requested, scrutinize them. As a sales engineer, manage requests without succumbing to fear or threats.

Challenge threats or demands by asking questions about why a change is required. Use these situations as opportunities to demonstrate professional management and diplomacy. Evaluate new requests based on their impact on PoC objectives and timelines.

## Know Your Audience

Expand your communication beyond core participants directly involved in the PoC. Identify and engage with individuals on the periphery (edge participants) who may not be central but can still influence decisions. Be attentive to casual mentions of these individuals in emails, meetings, or discussions.

Ask about their involvement, role, and importance within the company. Edge participants can often wield significant influence, so be mindful of their perspectives.

## Navigate the Political Landscape

Understand the politics surrounding a PoC. Some customers may oppose it or work against its success. Work constructively with individuals who may be hindering progress. Seek to build bridges with them, even if it poses challenges.

When politics becomes a factor, engage in discussions to understand opposing views. Create opportunities to align objectives or convert skeptics into supporters. Address these challenges early to prevent undermining your efforts later.

## Prioritize the Essential Tasks

Recognize that you can't accomplish everything in a PoC. Focus on essential tasks that drive the PoC forward, keeping the big picture in mind. Remember that a PoC is about illustrating your solution, not implementing it comprehensively or showcasing every feature.

Stay on track by focusing on a clearly defined set of success criteria specified in your PoC Agreement document.

## Avoid Workarounds

Whenever possible, stick to the off-the-shelf manufacture of your solution. Workarounds, while tempting in the heat of a PoC, may lead to long-term support challenges. Consider the implications before opting for a workaround, as the experience of sales engineers suggests that it tends to detract rather than benefit customers.

In summary, these principles, when applied with intention and adaptability, can significantly enhance the effectiveness of your Proof of Concept. By maintaining clarity, communication, and strategic focus, you pave the way for successful PoCs and lasting customer relationships.

## Conclusion

I am sure I could come up with more best practices – but these are the ones that arise most often. If you want to access further resources or want to share your own best practice then refer to the Final Comments and Resources section of the book. There you will find how to access our other online content sites and how to contact us.

# V

# Final Comments and Resources

# 13

# Final Comments

This marks the conclusion of the second edition of **The Essential Guide to Navigate Your Proof of Concept**. I eagerly anticipate connecting with sales engineers to receive their valuable feedback and contributions on this subject.

By incorporating insights from the sales engineering community, we ensure the ongoing relevance of this crucial practice in executing Proof of Concepts.

*Many of the updates came from various presales professionals to make us this second edition.* Thank you for all your comments, corrections, and content!

My primary objective in crafting this book is to inspire sales engineers to grasp the optimal methods for executing a Proof of Concept. As presales professionals, we must strive for a "world-class" level of engagement. Our actions, or lack thereof, within a sales engagement significantly impact the eventual outcome. Among the various practices at our disposal, the execution of a Proof of Concept stands out as a pivotal factor contributing to the success of closing opportunities.

Throughout this book, my constant refrain has been the importance of executing a Proof of Concept in a truly **world-class manner**. I trust that you've identified elements, practices, and mindsets within these pages that guide the execution of a Proof of Concept in that direction.

Another objective behind penning this book is to foster greater collaboration and engagement within the sales engineering community. If you possess ideas, approaches, tools, or feedback on how we can further enhance the practice of navigating a successful Proof of Concept,

```
I invite you to share your insights. Feel free to drop me a note,
comment, or idea. I look forward to getting your input.
```

**Continued success in your sales engineering career!**

# 14

# Resources

T hank you for purchasing this book and taking the time to read it. Its impossible to place all the content related to any subject in a single publication. If you want further information and resources then head on over to our online site under the banner of PoC Essentials.

PoC Essentials is our dedicated brand encompassing everything concerning evaluations and Proof of Concepts. Make PoC Essentials your primary destination for discovering other top-notch practices in the management of world-class evaluations, particularly proof of concepts.

*Feel free to reach out and connect with us for inquiries, questions, feedback, or to share your PoC stories.*

We can also work alongside your team to fine-tune and enable world-class PoC practices and mindsets. Contact us to learn about our coaching, courses, and consulting services.

## How To Connect With Us

- TGM Consulting Group - https://tgmconsultinggroup.com/
- PoC Essentials - https://tgmconsultinggroup.com/PoCessentials
- Contact Us: info@tgmconsultinggroup.com
- Book Meeting: https://tidycal.com/tonymatos
- LinkedIn: https://www.linkedin.com/in/tmatos/

PoC Essentials is a niche content site under my parent site TGM Consulting Group - which is a niche consulting group, *exclusively devoted to supporting presales professionals.*

## Our Mission

Empower your sales team, comprised of both sales engineers and sales leaders, to skillfully orchestrate and navigate evaluations that lead to success! Understand that an evaluation is not just a casual offering to customers; it should be a deliberate strategic decision and a key component of your team's overall sales strategy. It's essential to recognize that achieving success in an evaluation is not solely about technical prowess; it equally involves securing a sales victory.

At PoC Essentials, we specialize in providing consulting, coaching, and training to elevate your team's ability to execute world-class proof of concepts. Our online sites aim to provide you support whether from coaching, consulting, or content courses to empower you with skills and perspectives to navigate a world-class proof of concept.

Our broader objective is to socialize the mindset and practices of becoming a world-class presales professional. Discover more about our specialized consulting services by visiting https://tgmconsultinggroup.com/PoCessentials

# 15

# Seven Habits of Impactful Evaluations

## Free eBook!

I f you want to get a bird-eye view of Evaluations (another term used in place of Proof of Concept) then access this free ebook. It complements this book as well as being a great ice-breaker to share with your contacts, peers, and sales leadership.

This eBook is meant a concise business-level discussion of the mindsets and practices of world-class presales professionals to manage a PoC. Many have used this book to introduce these habits and practices to their team on how best to manage evaluations.

*You know how it is...sometimes hearing the same information you have been prompting from an external source gets people's attention.*

Go ahead and download a copy today!

## Download Your FREE eBook!

Just head on over to https://tgmconsultinggroup.com/sevenhabits to download your free copy!

Tony Matos

# Seven Habits
# of
# Impactful
# EVALUATIONS

IMPROVE YOUR WIN-RATE

*https://tgmconsultinggroup.com/sevenhabits*

# 16

# PoC Qualification Form

## Overview

The following is a detailed outline of the PoC Qualification Form. If you want to access a free copy of this then refer to the Resources section later in this book.

## Form Components

### Purpose

This is a standard description of the form's purpose, including identifying the vendor and customer name. You can and should adjust this to meet any organizational requirements.

### Customer Information

Capture general contact information regarding the company and primarily customer contacts for the PoC.

- Company name

- Contact name
- Contact email
- Contact information

## PoC Scope

The following content frames the details of the PoC. The customer should complete these details in their own words. The sales team should meet with a customer to ensure they provide you with their responses.

- Project Scope
- Current State
- Desired State
- Gap
- Working backward, when do you need something in place?
- Proposed PoC Start & End Date
- Success Criteria

## PoC Context

It is important to capture information including the competitive landscape, next steps, and the key decision-makers involved in the PoC. You also want to understand the path to purchase, including who, when, and how a solution will be acquired.

- Are you evaluating any other solutions?
- Assuming successful completion of the PoC meets your success criteria, what typically happens next?
- Provide contact information for the decision-makers
- The expected purchase date following a successful PoC?
- Is this project budgeted within the time frames specified?
- Do the decision-makers have project approval, or does that reside with someone else? If it resides with someone else, provide contact information

for the project approver.

## Vendor Information

The following information is internal and completed by the sales team. This information is essential to capture, as it provides the connection to your CRM.

- PoC opportunity information
- Which Sales Engineer(s) will manage this PoC?
- Account Manager name
- Account Manager email
- Sales Manager
- Sales Engineer manager
- CRM opportunity link
- Opportunity amount
- Identify any red flags along with any concerns and observations

Leverage the PoC Qualification form to initiate a discussion with your team and the customer regarding the need and feasibility of conducting an evaluation. Once you complete this form move to the next phase of making a decision based on the evidence and information you have collected via the form.

# More Information

If you want further information about this form or to discuss other PoC issues then drop me an email at info@tgmconsultinggroup.com. I look forward to hearing from you.

# About the Author

Tony Matos is committed to empowering professionals with essential skills, drawing upon his impressive 35-year career in IT and presales management. Throughout his journey, Tony has effectively led high-performing teams, honing his expertise in pivotal roles with industry giants like SAP, ORACLE, SAS, and Citrix.

The principles and practices Tony shares are not merely theoretical concepts; rather, they are battle-tested strategies developed over his extensive industry tenure. Tony's proficiency extends across sales engineering, sales engineering management, marketing automation, and team building. His primary focus lies in instilling best practices and employing intelligent methodologies to cultivate top-tier sales engineers. Discover Tony's insights, techniques, tools, and articles tailored for sales engineers on the PoC Essentials platform.

The strategies presented in this book have not only undergone rigorous field testing but have also been successfully implemented in Fortune 500 companies. Tony Matos brings a wealth of real-world experience to guide professionals toward excellence in their respective fields.

Contact Us: info@tgmconsultinggroup.com

Book Meeting: https://tidycal.com/tonymatos

**You can connect with me on:**
- https://tgmconsultinggroup.com
- https://tgmconsultinggroup.com/pocessentials
- https://www.linkedin.com/in/tmatos